What People Are Saying About Marilyn and Her Work!

Brilliant, profound, and to the point. This little book is a classic and will be read long after she is gone. I love how she writes.

Now that a couple of years have passed since we broke through 2012, it is even more significant. Don't underestimate this book, it haunts you over time, as the truth of the message becomes more and more revealed.

> *Linda Schiller-Hanna, Founder, Natural Psychic School of Metaphysics; Founder, Angel Love Healing Center; Speaker, :Edgar Cayce's ARE Intuition Trainer*

This little book is priceless. I found it to be one of the most valuable works I have ever read. I felt Marilyn Redmond speaking from her heart to mine about things she must have experienced because her book has "the ring of truth" that makes reading it like listening to a wise friend tell you things you've been searching for all your life.

I recommend that everyone who wants to live a more loving and honest life read this book, not just once, but study it and as far as possible, commit it to memory and use it to begin living at a higher level.

> *Lachlan Mitchell, Coexisting Disorder Coordinator, Bathurst Community Corrections Service, Australia*

Wonderful description of raising our vibration to Love. I found this book very enlightening and helpful in many ways. There is an explanation for questions about the shift from 3rd dimension through 4th and into the 5th, choosing to replace fear with LOVE, the highest vibration, and protecting our beautiful planet. Honoring nature. I highly recommend this book for clarity and much-needed guidance to save our planet, thus ourselves.

Jeannie Anderson, Reiki Master

It was truly inspirational and put a smile on my face. What a superbly wonderful book, beautifully written, composed and the message is pure and uplifting. Thank you for allowing me to work on this.

Lousie Atherton, editor of this book

The Real Meaning of 2012:
A New Paradigm Bringing Heaven to Earth

Marilyn L. Redmond
BA, CHT, IBRT

Dreamtime Press

Published by
Dreamtime Press
3290 Valley View Drive
Grand Junction, Colorado 81503
970-462-7132
Email: Publisher@DreamtimePress.com
Text Copyright © 2014 Marilyn Redmond
All rights reserved.

This book is printed on demand, so no copies will be remaindered or pulped.

ISBN No: 0982399987

Every effort has been made to give appropriate credit to copyright holders of works cited in this publication. If there are any inadvertent omissions, we apologize to those concerned. The publisher apologizes for any errors or omissions in this text and would be grateful for notification of any corrections that should be incorporated in future reprints or editions of this book. If you are the copyright holder of any uncredited work herein, please contact us at Publisher@DreamtimePress.com.

All rights reserved. No part of this publication may be reproduced in any material form (including photocopying or storing in any medium by electronic means and whether or not transiently or incidentally to some other use of this publication) without the written permission of the copyright holder except in accordance with the provisions of the Copyright, Designs, and Patents Act of 1988. Applications for the copyright holder's written permission to reproduce any part of this publication should be addressed to the publishers.

The purpose of this book is to educate and entertain. The author shall have neither liability nor responsibility to any person or entity.

Acknowledgements

I want to acknowledge my wonderful spiritual support team of my angels, ascended masters, and archangels. I was told to write this information during a channeling and to put it into a book. This knowledge is basic to the changes coming in our lives. It is transformative. My spiritual team provides the inspiration for all my writing, speaking, and channeling. Thank you for your assistance, upon which I can always depend.

Contents

The Third Dimension—The Physical 1

A Third Dimensional Picture 5

Changing Your Emotional Life 9

Understanding the Old Dynamics 15

What Is Changing? 19

Are You Ready to Make a Decision to Change? 21

How to Overcome the Ego 27

Moving Through the Fourth Dimension 35

Into the Fifth Dimension—2012 39

Celebration Time—Heaven on Earth 43

Life is Love: Affirmations for Living 47

Perfection 48

Afterward 49

The Third Dimension—The Physical

We call our surroundings the physical world. The earth as most of us perceives it today appears to be in three dimensions: length, width, and depth. We perceive material items that appear to have a form, weight, and are solid with our five senses. These items are observed through taste, touch, smell, sight, and hearing. Focusing on items made of matter has become customary and routine.

Our planet earth is made up of vibrational frequencies. It has different levels of slow and low vibrations ranging to high and faster speeds. In various levels of vibration are octaves of energy. Each person, animal, or place has its own vibration. It has consciousness or energy that is particular to its own rate of movement of this force that appears solid. Your reaction to experiences in the third dimension determines your mental, emotional, and spiritual life.

The vibrational scale of consciousness is much larger than our eyes can perceive or ears can hear. This includes lower negative sensations as those based in deeper fears, a slower dark pulse. There are higher tempos as joy, peace, and empowerment based in love and light in the highest vibrations. These levels of energy or spirit make up the emotional vibrational scale. There are levels of consciousness for all parts of our lives that fit somewhere in a massive range of vibrations.

Your reactions to the physical world come from your mindset or mental conditioning. Your mental attitudes produce your feelings. Negative thinking and actions offer lower emotions whereas positive ideas and conduct produce higher emotions.

Within the expanse of pulsing force, is Planet Earth in the third dimension. It was created in a higher range, often called grace. Over time, as humans descended into lower, denser energy, the planet fell from grace. This is, usually, called the "fall of man." When separated from the abundance, joy, and prosperity of grace, man tried to compensate for the missing inner contentment and fulfillment. Searching for outer material, wealth, and human power, to replace the missing inner peace, man has gradually, but ruthlessly, debased the riches of the planet through desecration of natural resources and toxic elements added to our foods, medicines, water, and air.

This fear-based perpetuation of "He who wins has all the toys," has brought poverty, hunger, and chaos. The survival of the fittest is an illusion, as an inner bankruptcy has become the real victor. The crisis and turmoil from insatiable motives brought lower vibrational energy that has almost destroyed the earth. These ideas perpetuated lower vibrational density even more.

By restoring the planet, our society and values are in the process of regeneration. By releasing old beliefs, ideas, and negative emotions, people are raising the planetary energy from a fear-based culture that has dominated all parts of the lives of the population. The consciousness of the earth is currently in the process of returning to its original state of being.

There has been a planetary cry from our dying Mother Earth for help. The greedy plundering and devastation that was draining the life force was bringing its demise. People have begun to raise their own energy into more loving vibrations by becoming better caretakers of the earth and its natural assets. Through this group effort, the planet will return to a higher vibration. The vibration is ascending, and with it so is planet Earth.

This rearranging of energy is occurring now. The turmoil in many countries, the crises of the financial world, the chaos in government affairs, are all part of the necessary shift for the fear based denser vibrational forces to rise to higher levels. This awakening offers the idea that fears should not control our lives. Rather it is time to move into enjoying life.

More and more, it is being proven, that material possessions and fortunes do not make a person wealthy in spirit. In fact, it can produce feelings of emotional insecurity. People are coming to realize that collecting, purchasing, and hoarding belongings does not bring happiness. Our government debt is symbolic of an inner spiritual bankruptcy. The illusion of a third-dimensional material utopia is crumbling. An unstable foundation will not sustain equitable abundance of prosperity. The old paradigm is collapsing.

That there is more to life than wealth for a select few is a new awakening. Learning that possessions and power are not part of reality, but come from the ego, opens new thinking and possibilities. An inner journey of what is not visible becomes a practical choice. This option becomes reasonable. Releasing what does not work, for what does work is rational. We were looking for our pie in the sky in all the wrong places.

How do you build a foundation that will sustain a bright life of love, trust, and understanding? How can we find unity, cooperation, and equality? Are prosperity, abundance, and well-being for all?

Moving into a new paradigm is the solution—one that offers fairness and thriving for all. Is that too outrageous to believe? I think not. Choosing to replace fear with love is a viable solution. It can provide a stable basis for a life that provides for the populace. The reality of truth, honesty, and compassion that emanates from love is what we have been looking for the whole time.

A Third Dimensional Picture

Three major reactions to the focuses around us that may produce a lack of well-being are scarcity, insecurity, and self-centeredness. These come from negative perception when we observe our situations. In fact, they are encouraged by the media, advertising, entertainment, even medical, and religious elements. A barrage of stressful messages fills our daily lives. Living in fear produces emotional insecurity. Living in this lower vibrational environment is eventually fatal. Most medical conditions are a direct result of a toxic, rather than a nurturing, vital power in our lives and our minds.

Most humans regard food and shelter as necessary. Our current ideas of survival today depend on money, jobs, and savings. Therefore, the lack of work or shortage of funds becomes more threatening. This creates a feeling of scarcity.

Survival of the fittest, strongest, and wealthiest has become the aim. Scarcity elicits the conclusion that someone has to go without. Is this a valid assumption? These conditions draw reactions of competition and conflict, rather than sharing and cooperating. However, encouraging an equitable environment and spreading the wealth is seen as socialistic. It is seen as an opposing thought, rather than one, which can work in conjunction to create a better world and individual life.

Often, money and relationships create the most difficulties for people, especially if there is a neediness for another to support us, take care of us, or provide companionship. Relationships bring attachment that is more emotional through the risk of rejection or abandonment. These concerns convey insecure feelings. What has been lost is self-confidence, self-realization, in other words, the self that is your inner essence of well-being.

As wealth has accumulated into the hands of the few, many people are feeling less secure. Financial insecurity is growing and increasing. Buying ability has been reduced by less available jobs and therefore less income to purchase the essentials. There is no opportunity to save for misfortune, the future, and old age. Is it possible to rebuild under present circumstances?

When people are afraid for their lives from threatening outside forces and economic conditions, fear creates self-centeredness and powerless victims. Additional negative feelings increase from violent games, movies, news media, and actual crimes. This fear-based life has become the norm over thousands of years.

There are threats of war by terrorist organizations that are used as an excuse to reduce the freedoms of the individual. Insecurity, a lack of individual autonomy, and powerlessness is intimidating. This brings domination and manipulation over the people. In addition, reducing the population through genetically engineered food and medicines, as well as the added toxins in the air and water, makes it easier to control the population. Created conflict with one country, culture, or religion and another causes the predicament of division and not unity.

The perception of the above events, by the ego, creates a reaction of fear and survival. Self- interest is the motivation for becoming the fittest. The means are adapted to justify the ends, with deceptive wars, narrow-minded loyalties, and the news' sources restricted to propaganda for the good of the few who want to rule the planet.

Those that question or object, become the insurgent, as a few at the top cunningly promote their agenda to reduce the personal freedoms of the people, rather than uphold our Constitution. Surveillance cameras and Patriot's Acts take away the inalienable rights of the people. The Congress, at the mercy of their financial benefactors, only allows the crumbs to come down to their constituents, as the cream rises to fill the pockets of the rich.

The American dream was a mirage to divert attention to the real circumstances behind the big green curtain as in The Wizard of Oz. With major debt in the government and empty pockets in the general population, loss of income from outsourcing, computerization, and mechanization, the people have taken to the Occupy Movement and other such actions.

Is there hope of a new economy of co-operation and sharing with well-being coming to replace the old paradigm? Will releasing old energy of negativity from the past, and replacing it with a rising energy of love, create a new prototype? Will the maladies of disease, old age, want, and poverty be dispelled with grace? Is the solution instead to embrace divine qualities of forgiveness for the perpetrators of our collapse and seek peace and harmony with all? Is there a transformation occurring to birth a new paradigm?

The reality of this scheme to fuel scarcity, competition, and exclusiveness through exploitation is slowly being revealed. Seeing past false premises that have been sold to society and forced on us has brought rejection and awakening. Rebellion by the 99% against the 1% is in progress. The veils that covered the eyes of the 99% are falling from their eyes and revealing the deception and maneuvers behind the scenes.

Changing Your Emotional Life

Since your emotional life is the focus that attracts what you receive, it is best to understand and address this less understood part of our existence. The Map of Consciousness, (Illustration 1) about levels of vibrations offers labels for your emotions. Please note, the negative terms used under the column for the God view are not judgmental or critically intended. They are to identify the level of energy that humans may emanate from their subconscious and can influence their progression upward. Emotions, vibrations, and energy are different terms for spirit. Where your energy resides is the level of your consciousness. Is it possible to raise your consciousness?

Feelings reveal the level of your consciousness by being positive or negative, such as forgiveness or regret on the chart. As your consciousness rises, feelings move up the scale of emotions towards joy. This is possible when your attitudes begin to move out of trauma, drama, or chaos.

Each time you move higher on the scale of emotions, you feel relief. It is a systematic process. Emotions are your guidance to where you are in moving beyond your dread, anxiety, and frustrations. The goal is to attain self-realization and enlightenment.

It is not practical to shift your energy from the bottom to the top all at once, as shown on the illustration, because the human body cannot handle such a drastic change in one single leap. Do not try such giant steps of advancement by yourself. This could create too many problems emotionally to handle at once. Small, simple steps bring you closer to your goal in a more comfortable, balanced way.

Vibrational Scale of Consciousness

Releasing old emotions, as the new ones become your focus, should be a moderate process. This can be compared to grieving a death when grieving old ideas, dreams and desires, and slowly letting go of thoughts and feelings. Unresolved grief is a major cause of illness and being stuck. It is important to acknowledge and mourn your old pains. An inner house cleaning is needed for completely rising above negative energy.

Emotions need to flow. As when they are obstructed, they become medical, emotional, and physical problems. Accepting changes allows blocked energy to move again throughout out the body. The life giving energy of emotions nurtures the spiritual body just as the flow of blood feeds our physical body. Acupuncture, Chiropractic, Qigong, and flower essences can be valuable to support the energy flowing in the body. They are more effective than often realized by current thinking.

Moving into a new paradigm means that the body will be restored to healthy functioning. Prescription drugs, toxic thinking, and negative emotions all block this energy flow. It is wise to stop the use of chemicals such as MSG, sugar substitutes, and fluoride—all toxic substances—these products act as poisons in your body.

Eating organic foods, rather than genetically altered foods, manufactured and sold in boxes or frozen pre-made dishes with preservatives, are better for you. Your thinking, well-being, and feelings will improve.

Changing Your Life to a Spiritual One

In addition to eliminating toxic chemicals from your life, it is necessary to consider releasing negative emotions and thoughts. You will have been conditioned by past events and calamities throughout your life. This focus keeps you from being present in the "NOW."

Resentments, anger, and other negative feelings are triggers that bring up past emotional experiences. This continues to reinforce depressing, pessimistic, and harmful feelings and behavior in the present. Letting go of these negative feelings and emotions brings loving awareness of the bigger picture, which in turn shows you the possibility of a more positive life. When you learn from your mistakes, wisdom will come.

As you acknowledge the other persons for playing their role for you to learn your lesson, you also acknowledge yourself for needing this experience to grow. Your awareness is freedom. You will move more fully from your past into the "Now" with each life lesson.

While having a foot in the old crisis and turmoil, often your other foot is in the worry zone about your future needs. This dual thinking keeps you in fantasyland. Living in the past or future, projects a neediness or insecurity. You have no energy left to live the life that is in front of you. This drains energy from your body, which produces health problems.

It is easy to understand that you cannot have a better past. In addition, you cannot change the future as it has not happened yet and is, therefore, a fantasy. Moving into the present becomes the only practical option. You are grounded in the "Now." You can make powerful new decisions, make changes, and new experiences can happen. You can move forward into a better life, and thus, the future will be fine without worrying about it.

God is always with you— the only power. The presence of God is the most important power in your life. The past and future do not exist. You let go of the old idea of a punishing God and negative experiences. You now put your faith in a positive solution and your "being" in the moment.

You had previously accepted without question the opinions, beliefs, and theories of others who were authorities in your life. Now there is evidence of an infinite power of good.

Omnipresent means the spiritual presence of a Higher Power is always with us and fills all spaces. All we ever have is the presence of right now. It knows your needs before you do and goes before you to make your path straight. That means the past and the future have no power, but are instead an illusion. There is nothing outside the oneness of God. The ability to enjoy and change—shift energy— occurs in the reality of "Now."

Omnipotent means all-powerful. Be still and know that I am God is often misunderstood. You and your Father are one. That means that the "I" inside of you is the Father. That God resides within because the Kingdom of God is within you, is not stressed in religion. That power is present with you for your guidance through your thoughts and feelings. You have the courage to do what is necessary and right.

Omniscient means all-knowing. As you view each life experience from a new and positive perspective, you come more and more into God consciousness. You are listening to that still, small voice inside of you that is God. Freedom comes with an understanding that below our accepted idea of what comprises our consciousness —God consciousness is already there. It has only been hidden by our human way of thinking. God composes the consciousness of an individual, our identity. It is the creative source, presence, power, principle, and cause. Understanding this meaning of consciousness realizes the secret of life. You move beyond accepted knowledge, finding balance, harmony, and life eternal.

Understanding the Old Dynamics

It is useful to have a new view of how a third-dimensional world exists. As we come to earth to experience the third dimension, we live in the denser energy of this planet and our birthright seems to be blindness to the awareness of God consciousness. We need to experience the Spirit in God's love. However, as humans we have been taught that we are separated from God through church dogma. However, it is the ego— edging God out— that is separated from God consciousness. It is our job, therefore, to learn how to live totally in God-consciousness at the demise of the ego. We come to earth with a job to do, but we are, usually, unaware that we are to find our way back to total God-consciousness.

Think of yourself within a sea of spiritual energy. You realize as an incoming soul that you need data existing in your new surroundings. The ego, the part that has separated for information in the third dimensional, material world, can be likened to a periscope on a submarine. It extends out looking for feedback. As a new individual, how do you meet your needs, the basic survival instincts that are inbuilt within humans? They are to nurture and to find food, and shelter. Your life now becomes a search for the answers to these questions. The need to gain information to maintain life in the third dimension continues the ego's purpose.

As we learn in this new dimension, the negative teaches us the most. Either we are nurtured and have our needs met, or we are denied, often unjustly punished and frequently left to our own devices. We are not even aware of the dynamics that direct this, as we cannot see it. If our needs are not met as helpless entities, it is natural to blame our caretakers for the deficiencies of our existence. As we grow and mature, we project from ourselves the neediness, the anger, and all the other emotions that represent our insecurities. If our needs are met, we automatically grow in God consciousness.

Unaware that the core of each individual is being projected outside of himself or herself, it is easy not to see your own faults. Not taking responsibility for your faults, you only want to accept the good parts of yourself until denial becomes a way of life. Therefore, seeing only the good qualities and not accepting your mistakes, is a partial view, and you do not see yourself as a whole.

As we mature, the data we are picking up with our periscope becomes a reflection of our own inadequacies and we react. This perpetuates the negative energy that we continue to emit. We are unknowingly, our own worst enemy. Until we transform the negative to positive with love, this cycle can repeatedly occur in any lifetime. Each time is more painful. These grow over time to bring a lack of self-esteem and emotional insecurity.

Difficulties with your relationships and employment problems are also ways to identify that your life is not in harmony. Illness or calamities are wake up calls that the body is out of balance or resisting the light. The ego is doing its job, and you are buying into it. Your life is not in accord with your dreams and desires. Fighting a predicament is resistance to reality. With a closed and narrow mind, including a lack of honesty, life seems hopeless and helpless.

In ignoring these circumstances caused by a fear-based attitude, it keeps you down in the darkness of lower energy. This brings disease, usually, depression, and other difficulties. Most people live in the dark because it is familiar or within their comfort zone to stay, in what they deem, "safe." Society supports staying in lower density because the powerless person is easier to control and manipulate. Medicating this condition only increases the lack of clarity and low energy. Only when it is too painful do you recognize there is a problem. It is then that people are encouraged to drug it through prescriptions, alcohol, or other addictions and not face the actual truth.

If you try any short-term approaches, they, usually, do not last; the approach was not a change in lifestyle. You find yourself back with the same problems or additional ones that, in fact, make more difficulties. Remaining a victim, looking for someone to save you, does not work. You may try many affirmations and reading books to change, but they only address the symptoms and therefore all are superficial until there is an inner change.

Other people are your mirror; however, you choose to see the parts in them that make you comfortable. It is easy to have friends who have similar tastes, and those who are not in agreement with you become your enemy. However, they are showing you what needs to be healed in you. Your faults and mistakes need improvement to heal you into wholeness.

Running away from reality is common. Alcoholism, Alzheimer's, Schizophrenia, Bipolar Disorder, and other illnesses are terms labeling people who do not feel their inner pain. Often the suffering person attracts others to enable their problems. We set up huge organizations to raise millions of dollars to eradicate these apparent diseases and never address the real causes. As a society, we encourage sympathy by looking to medicine for solutions. The basis of their problems has nothing to do with the physical and cannot be healed with any drug.

It, usually, takes a crisis to bring enough courage to change yourself, to find a better way. Your cry for help is heard when you reach despair and express a meaningful need. Your life will change. Most people do not just decide on a new life style without some tragedy. It takes deep motivation such as illness, a threatened life, or a disaster, to change. It has to be more than an intellectual resolution. The solutions must come from the heart as well as the head. The head/ego does not want to lose its dominion over your life.

What Is Changing?

The help that our planet called out for is finally coming right now. More energy has been coming in to raise the planet's vibrations out of negativity and denser energy, which ultimately brings death. The planet is more alive today. Though still heavily polluted, more light is being sent to the earth to raise its consciousness. The consciousness of earth is returning to a loving planet as it was intended to be.

People are supporting this rising of energy with such spiritual practices as meditation, helping others through volunteering, and participating in causes to improve the environment. More and more people are supportive of the homeless, those without jobs, and those without medical insurance. The attitudes of people are coming into positive ways of cooperating in community efforts to maintain and retain healthy environments. New environmental laws are being passed, and many are speaking out for clean water.

People are taking action to bring change where they can by withdrawing funds from commercial banks that are installing multiple unfair charges and making millions at their customers' expense. Customers are transferring money to credit unions and low or non-profit institutions. Many people now deposit cash into funds for those in desperate need due to disasters.

People are recognizing that the news and media are not telling the whole story about changes going on around the world and in this country. Instead, people are using the internet to seek out accurate and truthful information. Activities by whistle blowers that disclose hidden deceptions, lies about government activities, and writers that reveal the truth about century old history are becoming increasingly more commonplace. The Wiki Leaks Scandal is only the tip of the iceberg. As higher energy is replacing lies of the past, fantasy is dispelling, and reality is finally being exposed. The truth can set us free of the control and manipulation of the past.

Are You Ready to Make a Decision to Change?

Are you up to the ordeal? Reducing the influence of the ego and returning to God-consciousness in your life is not an easy task. The change is not for the faint-hearted. With every step, there will be resistance from the ego. However, this is achievable at this time.

Taking the challenge to release all the fear-based energy takes faith. You can return to the higher vibrations of light and love; it is available right now. At this time in history, there is an opportunity to undo the false power of the ego and reinstate your real essence of Love and being loved. Restoring your true nature as a spiritual being in the image of your Creator is the goal. This is a real "journey of the soul." This is ascension.

If you choose to take this mission, it is not impossible. However, there will need to be an inner housecleaning of your old fear, guilt, and shame. In addition, resentments, anger, and other negative emotions need releasing, and there must be forgiveness. Filling the new void from clearing out the ego's negative survival messages is a process. Compassion needs to replace your old feelings.

This is not a scholarly procedure, but a spiritual journey to travel. It is a choice to move from your head into your heart for intuitive information. Restoring the splintered wounded parts of your soul with love is a journey to balance your energy from your karmic past.

The perceptions of the ego saw your negative character flaws still needing healing from what you sowed in the past. As the lower energy is allowed to leave your awareness, there now is space to allow positive higher vibrations of love, kindness, and patience to replace the influence of the ego and rise into higher consciousness. You now can sow love instead of your fears and reap the unlimited and almighty harvest. You will ascend out of the negative denser energy of the ego.

Before we incarnate on earth, we agree to play certain parts in people's lives as well as our own. The environments and people around you are mirrors to reflect back the specific ills that need identification. They act out the attitudes and mindsets for you to recognize specific shortcomings that need to be forgiven in others, as well as yourself, and loved back into wholeness.

Denial is not a river in Egypt, but the lack of taking responsibility to right the wrongs from your own actions, now or in the past. Being rigorously honest that you played a part in the circumstances is sometimes not easy to accept. The truth can be painful. However, realistically, it takes two people to interact. It requires both people engaged, to generate a conflict. What was your part or mistake?

Therefore, one person is not the only cause of a relationship dilemma. Most people fight to the end to be right. There is conflict when someone does not feel his or her needs are met. Unwittingly, both add to the trouble by needing to be right, having their way, or winning the argument.

A mature person allows others to have an opinion that differs. This is the real power from within. However, in truth, the one who uses passive resistance is the winner and is more powerful. The ego does not like to have the truth of the situation determined as it loses power when this happens. If one person steps back from the conflict and decides they do not have to win, the other person feels they have the power.

The apparent winner is in the ego's illusion that there is a victory. Needing to be in charge because someone else might be more powerful, richer, or more intelligent is threatening and superficial. Continuing in the path of proving that you have all the answers and know what is best for others is controlling and manipulating. This is the game of the ego. It is a fantasy, an illusion, into which people buy.

Forcing situations to meet demands, subtly or obviously, overwhelms and victimizes so that it becomes a game of who has the power or wealth. The ego needs this false sense of power for survival. People push hard to sustain this authority and influence. It is a passive-aggressive game. When children play "King of the Mountain," they are acting out the same dynamics that they see in their parents and others.

This passive-aggressive game distracts people from the reality of the love inside. It diverts the focus on the truth of who you are. The ego's game is deceptive as it digs into darker energy and becomes a downward spiral repeating itself more painfully. The result is that medical conditions arise from not having a loving vital force flowing through your body; it advances illness, incompatibility, and other difficulties. The pain and misery drain the enthusiasm for enjoying life. This delights the ego, as it has a false reason to exist.

As your emotional energy descends into lower density vibrations of negativity, it dominates your attitude, thinking, and actions. These fear-based feelings keep the darkness intact from hope, help, or overcoming the circumstances. Childish resentments become the obsessive focus and keep you in a fantasy that it is others that should change. Selfishness, dishonesty and self-seeking are like a boomerang that returns more misery. Reaping what you sow can be wretched. You become spiritually bankrupt.

If you have hit the bottom of your emotional life and have become desperate, there are few options, mainly suicide or death. You cannot see any opportunities to move up and out of this bleak existence and choose to remove yourself from a life that seems like hell. You may have a death wish subconsciously, or actions are bringing you closer to death, as in taking illegal drugs or prescriptions, which are simply poisons by a different label. Another option is to become so sick that you die from an illness, like having cancer. Some doctors say that cancer is a socially acceptable way to die. Most illness is a slow death, especially with the toxic procedures of medicine. Emotionally the person gives up, and physical death is the result.

Most people do not understand if you commit suicide that you return to live that same life again until you learn the same lessons. This happens when you die from an illness. The consciousness you have when you leave this life will continue on your return. You have not evaded the lessons of your soul.

With an intervention, whether spiritual or from friends, a rude awakening occurs, that you need to change. Continuing in the old life style is no longer doable.

Do you choose to live or die?

Although the ego will continue to project your broken soul, now you have a chance to ignore it and look for a higher power to restore your sanity. Hitting rock bottom brought you to choosing a new path or life style. With surrender, new opportunities appear. There is another way.

With the choice not to continue your old immature ego ways, you can release that past emotional baggage, including your resentments, revenge, and guilt. You can choose to respond instead of react, breaking the old cycle of being a victim. This is the path out of the darkness of the lower energy perpetuated by the ego. This is growing into maturity.

Remember the ego separates your emotional connection from God, so the solution is to return to God. Choose positive over negative in your life. Refuse to buy into the fear mongers, societal false beliefs, or pessimistic family loyalty. These are of the ego. God has always been there, even if you focused elsewhere. God never left your consciousness. Who moved? Only you moved your focus to the ego's information from the five senses and only you can restore your attention back to the God within.

There are layers of false beliefs, deceit, and denial to identify. With total honesty, a new perspective will appear. Replacing your old ideas with love and grace offers you a new pair of glasses. You will see the light at the end of the tunnel!

The more love you allow into your thoughts, words, and actions, the more the ego diminishes. Replacing more and more with God by means of less and less of your selfish, immature attitudes and behaviors becomes the softer, easier way of life. You can stop anytime in any situation and reason things out as to the best, most loving, approach for you and the other person. This is Letting go and Letting God in.

No one is left out of this reprieve. It is your choice to accept the solution. Love is the answer. "All we need is love" becomes real.

How to Overcome the Ego

Science says that energy moves. In humans, we call this power our emotions. It is all about raising vibrational energy. See the chart that shows rising vibrations (the last column) that brings us closer to divinity and one with the Divine.

Taken from: The Formation of a Solar System-continued

World No.	Interpenetrating Worlds		Deity Impulse Number	Bubbles Per Atom	Worlds Vibration Rate
	World Name	Manifestation			
1st	Divine	Not yet reached by human mind	0	1	Hi Octaves
2nd	Nomadic	Nomads, sparks of the divine	1	49	↑
3rd	Spiritual	Highest spirit in man	2	2,401	
4th	Intuitional	Source of highest intuitions	3	117,649	
5th	Mental	Source of human mind	4	5.765 Million	
6th	Astral (emotional)	Emotions of man	5	282.5 Million	↓
7th	Physical	Physical	6	13.841 Billion	Low Octaves

Courtesy of Mack Van Wyk

Ending the energy drain from past issues elevates you to a height of God consciousness, love, or healthy vibrations of well-being. For me, spirituality means living in love or positive vibrations of energy that are called spirit.

The material world is tempting. It is used by the ego to promote your attraction, your use of time, and energy. A fancy house, a better job, or a new computer game can all be great distractions and deterrents and take your time away from what is of spiritual value if you let it. However, that joy is quick and fleeting. Does it really provide contentment, serenity, or inner peace? Do you keep buying something more, trying to find the one item or a person that will fill the emptiness inside?

Is it time to look for being genuine from your heart, rather than superficial from your ego? Material items are not of permanent value. The ego encourages you to buy one more thing to make you happy; however, they can break at any time. Many people looking for jobs used to have a great salary, beautiful home and yard, or a super car, but they are gone when the job is eliminated. They are temporary and cannot fulfill the missing void.

So what does bring reality, sanity, and serenity to your life? With your new decision not to follow in the path of the ego, it is time to replace your insanity from the material world that lures you with a false sense of pleasure. It becomes more obvious that your inner journey that focuses on sincerity with unconditional love will provide the fulfillment you desire. You are moving from your head into your heart.

Now your journey is an inner path of faith. Men of faith have courage. Releasing the outcome of each part of your life, allows a higher power to produce the outcomes that may even be better than what you intended. Leaving the results up to the Creator, who provides relief from your playing God in your life, and in the lives of your loved ones, lightens your burdens. You must trust the Universe/God to supply your needs and bring appropriate results into your life. This is real faith. If you do the footwork then turn the results over to your Creator; you will be surprised. It may be better than you imagined.

This higher power is an energy force; it is called by many labels such as Love, God, Creator, or Creative Forces. It cares for you. Relying on a power greater than you, replaces the ego, and it selfishness. You move into a higher consciousness of being more rational, loving, and sane.

Faith is powerful; it provides strength in your life. It is always there. It connects you to the positive stream of energy that created the universe. It supports you in all things. You are not alone trying to survive on the planet.

Contempt before investigation is of the ego. Investigate the fear with faith. Faith replaces fear when examining beyond the unknown. Now you have facts upon which to base a new decision. Will the details provide more understanding, so apprehension is not necessary? Yes, looking beyond the fear is faith.

As you become honest with yourself and move into this new place, opportunities appear. Honesty has replaced your denial. You move into a greater reality the more honest you become. You see from a new perspective. You are no longer separated from God as you move into new circumstances. Honesty directly connects you to a positive energy force, which dispels the darkness of the ego. Your feelings lighten. You feel good in the presence of God. Honesty has become the best policy.

With faith, you can now live in sincerity, honesty, and detachment. Detachment comes with facing your fears, releasing them and letting go of all negative emotions and situations. Sincerity comes from the heart. These are the keys to move out of the ego's influence. Now your faith is in those things that connect you to a Higher Power.

Another way to prevail over the ego is with information. Why be fearful of the unknown? Fear of the unknown disappears as you gain in understanding or knowledge. When you have information, there is no need for fear. This knowing replaces the unknown. When you know the original basis for the ego is separation from God, your thinking can change.

You learn to pray for your enemies. When a fearful situation arises, pray for that person or circumstance to culminate in the highest good for all. When you send out love, you smooth the path. You are not creating more chaos, but instead are sending loving energy that allows loving energy to return to you. Sending prayer or love is a very practical way to dispel the ego's influence of promoting turmoil and havoc. If someone does not feel threatened, the outcome can be very beneficial for all. They too are children of God.

When you are able to send love to others, do not forget to love yourself. This is often more difficult as so often the ego has influenced our lack of self-esteem and emotional insecurity. Some people have lived in guilt or shame for many reasons. They find it comfortable and normal to be this way. As you come to understand that you are made in the image of your Creator, the ego's messages of old can be forgotten as ancient history. The real you, the God-conscious person, can evolve into claiming your birthright. You are a child of God.

Another major way to prevail over the ego is through forgiveness. This is the bridge between the ego and your higher self. You extend forgiveness not because you approve of the other person's actions or attitudes, but because you no longer need to carry the emotional baggage. It is like releasing the shackles of the past. The event or predicament did happen; however, you can now perceive it from your higher self and acknowledge the other person is also a child of God.

You release the emotional distress of the past for a new today. Giving up the past to live in the 'Now' is freeing. You do it to liberate yourself from hanging on to something that is over, although it is presented as a learning experience necessary for your soul growth. Lessons in life are not always pleasant. In fact, you may have been through trials and tribulations that were horrifying. Now you discover your lessons learned through your experiences have fostered growth. This raises your energy into a higher consciousness. This is what life is about.

Others played out their part in our lessons. You asked them to help you before you were born into this life, with the experiences you needed to heal your soul. They volunteered to be in your play. They offered an opportunity for you to learn love, forgiveness, compassion, and gratitude. Taking responsibility for the karma we created is a major step in being accountable and balanced. Sending love to those problems, or people, we harmed in our past needs to be done.

You need to change this low energy of the ego to a higher vibration for you to move into a higher consciousness. With the ascension on our doorstep, forgiving our past predicaments becomes essential to raising our energy. The people who volunteered to play a part in our life did us a favor by providing the happening so that your energy could shift to a higher plane. There can be no negative energy in the Fifth dimension. Now you can move on and not be stuck in this old karma, bitterness, or resentment.

It is also necessary to stop blaming or judging others for your problems. This is a common occurrence from the ego. When you point a finger at someone else, there are several fingers pointing back at you. The only person you are inconsiderate of is yourself, when you do not take responsibility for your life. What you send out will come back to you.

Clearing out your past negative emotions, actions, and communications, you can return to being as one with your Creator. Taking responsibility for your life, and every part that you needed for your soul growth, is essential. Only when you respond in love to all situations that occur instead of reacting in revenge, hatred, or resentment towards others or internalizing guilt and shame, can you become a master of your emotions.

Now you have realized that no one else can save you. You save yourself from your ego. There is no devil, Satan, or hell. You have found that you are the cause and effect in your life. What you caused, comes back to be loved. When it comes sometimes so painfully, it is easy to run away physically or emotionally. Most people run from their consequences, which leads them further away from truth and love. We must all face reality.

When you attack someone else because of your fear, the other person will defend himself or herself and retaliate. When you are in a difficult situation, sending love will change the dynamics, and peace can be restored. No one can attack love. There is no threat from love. It is only ego's lie that we will be punished if we reveal our true self to God. The truth is that in surrendering to God, you have the love of God to protect you from any harm. It is the safest place to be.

The scariest thing in life is to be totally available to God's love. The ego had shut you down from love when you felt danger. The body closed off all light of God as a way to protect you from harm. When you are a child, this may be necessary to survive in an abusive and/or dangerous environment. However, as an adult, the ego continues to keep you from opening yourself up to your loving essence. Until the past is healed, we cannot be open to experiencing God's love.

Moving Through the Fourth Dimension

The role of the ego was to protect and inform you in the third dimension. It will try to dissuade you from pursuing higher aspects and attributes of your consciousness. However, with the coming Golden Age, the ego's influence must be loved into wholeness and fully integrated with all aspects of yourself.

The Fourth Dimension is the transition between Third and Fifth Dimensions. It is the rising of vibrations into more and more awareness of God and less of self. Becoming God-conscious opens up the Fourth Dimension to move out of ego based perceptions and begins your return to wholeness. With the decision to turn your life over to a Higher Power, you make a commitment to become a love-based person focused on the God of your definition. This choice moves you from an ego driven, fear based life to one of love. As you transform more and more of your ego self, you move higher in consciousness towards your Creator.

You may find yourself acting in new ways. You appreciate the gifts around you. Gradually, you are happier because now you recognize and comprehend situations as you never have before. As the denials leave, the clarity of vision becomes more obvious. The "aha's" begin to come. New activities appear for you to try. Maybe you are more generous or say something kind, whereas before you would have been too fearful. Your life begins to open up into more opportunities. New friends appear that are also growing on this spiritual path. You realize that you are changing. You will notice that each day will be different from your earlier occurrences. Your gratitude will expand. You are in the Fourth Dimension.

Your old negative behaviors and thinking do not appeal to you anymore. Past actions do not sit well now. You do not want to recreate that misery of the past. You are trying different solutions for your medical conditions that are now becoming more commonly accepted. Life has gone in a new direction, and you cannot go back.

Your focus is listening to your intuition, meditating, and reading spiritual books. You seem to want to learn more and search for those who have been down this path as a guide or teacher. You feel good about this. Listening to your heart instead of your head is becoming more habitual and routine.

You are not the same person who made the decision to change. Over time, it has happened. You trust the universe will take care of you as you experience difficult relationships, job challenges, and financial stress. Even when something does not go well, you have faith that as it works out, the results will be suitable. You acquire confidence in yourself. The sooner you accept the new open-minded ideas or experiences, the faster your progress is. You realize that only you can stop your growth to a higher Consciousness.

You feel different inside. The inner emptiness is not so empty. There is integrity as your insides match your outsides. People begin to trust and respect you. There is a sense of self-esteem and success. With God's help, your emotional security strengthens like you never experienced before. You can speak up for yourself in awkward situations. Awareness that it is all good becomes common in your thinking.

You "know" who you are now. Your beliefs and old ideas have left. You know your purpose. You think for yourself instead of parrot what you were taught by your family, in church, or by medicine. You know your natural state is love, health, and abundance. Becoming emotionally available is the "New You."

Your health has been improving. The balance is returning in your life as harmony is restored throughout your body. At this point, your spiritual life will change. You can change your emotions from negative to positive by changing your focus and releasing the negative feelings. You substitute the positive for the negative. You can meditate and hear the silent voice inside. Its guidance becomes stronger, and you begin to listen to the silent voice inside—you are a good person.

You become more aware of spiritual feedback. You have moved into the world of spirit. You might even see the spirit. With this transformation, it is possible to channel information for others if you choose to.

This is the highest a person in human form can achieve before moving into the Fifth Dimension of grace. The process of replacing the lower dense energy of the ego with the fruits of the spirit is the spiritual journey.

"The fruits of the spirit of the Christ are love, joy, obedience, long-suffering, brotherly love, kindness. Against such, there is no law. The spirit of hate, the anti-Christ, is contention, strife, faultfinding, lovers of self, lovers of praise. Those are the anti-Christ, and take possession of groups, masses, and show themselves even in the lives of men." #281-16 *Edgar Cayce*

It is important that we truly step up our own frequencies by assimilating cosmic energies, then learning to step more, and more into our 'soul' potential of wholeness, and heal the soul wounds that are keeping us from stepping into our own greatness.

By the time you arrive at this new level of higher consciousness, you enter what is often called 'Christ consciousness.' This is as high as we go before merging back into the Oneness. You have emotionally become open to all of God. You do not have to die physically to accomplish this for the first time in history. With your new higher Christ-consciousness, you are ready for ascension. This is a miraculous time to be alive and well and on our planet.

Into the Fifth Dimension—2012

It is necessary to open your heart chakra completely, letting your heart rule your mind, and not the vice versa. Balance is created through the unified energy centers of the chakras. With your action as 'co-creator' you move into a higher consciousness.

On December 21, 2012, a new door or portal opened into a level of realization that only a few have experienced throughout time. The ascended masters who have gone before us are now here preparing the way for our walk into this paradise. Many share their messages through channelers or in books that are channeled. They are here to assist you to find your self-realization of higher consciousness. You are on your way home.

In the Fifth Dimension, you move into grace. The Bible describes this as the 1000 years of peace. Satan is bound because negative, lower energy cannot sustain in higher vibrations. Those that have released all their old dark energy, tensions, and stresses will thrive in this new elevated experience with high-minded companions. Are you ready?

In this new paradigm, there will be no fearful or worried reactions that stop the Christ light from emanating. This is not a graduation, but another level to practice being your true God self. This is an opportunity to apply love in all parts of our lives. The inner light of who you are, is now unobstructed to radiate out to others. Let your light shine.

This is not the time to talk about it, but to "do it." Each challenge that appears causes us to respond in a loving way. The most visible of ascended masters, Jesus, exemplified living in this glory.

This journey continues into higher dimensions as you gradually become more spirit and less physically human. Your DNA will operate as originally intended. During this time, you will apply the principles of honesty, faith, and integrity. In addition, humility, increased spiritual awareness, and being of service, will become more your goals. This extending of your true self offers unity, community, and sharing.

There is a beautiful and true story about the Special Olympics that depicts the new attitude of the Fifth Dimension. This event took place in Seattle, Washington. The contest that stood out was the 100-yard dash. All the runners lined up with great enthusiasm. They all took off except for one runner who quickly tripped, fell, and began to cry. All of the other athletes stopped; they heard him. They came back and helped him up. They locked arms, and all went across the finish line together. The crowd cheered for 10 minutes. This demonstrates how humanity can get things done. We can transcend differences.

We work together and pool our creative energy and focus to accomplish amazing things. This happens on a local, as well as an international, level. Remember in 2010 when the Cuban miners were trapped for over 60 days? The international community joined and once again pooled creative energies, resources, and focus, going through a fair amount of challenge to get those miners out.

We have been going through new challenges to create this new earth. The significance of 2012 is prominent on the Internet and other social media, such as books, magazine articles, and seminars. There is much information available on the shift and transformation. Sometimes it is referred to by the term 'ascension'.

Earth and humanity are moving from a third-dimensional paradigm through the fourth dimension into a fifth-dimensional paradigm and then higher. We are moving away from a paradigm of separateness to a paradigm of togetherness. We are moving away from war, disease, and greed. In addition, we are rising above illness, oppression, poverty, and pollution. We are moving toward a place where all beings, including Mother Earth, will flourish. The theme is peace, harmony, and love.

There will be more challenges. With faith instilled with all individuals, we can do this well. Let us lock our arms together and create this new world.

Celebration Time—Heaven on Earth

2012 marks the end of one age and the beginning of a grand new one for humanity. This will be the greatest of all – the Golden Age. The golden rule will become common. Love your neighbor, as yourself, becomes a way of life. Loving your God with all your heart, mind, and soul becomes who you are. The First Commandment is being manifested as there are no other Gods; it has become real and not just words.

How has this happened? They have spiritualized inside of you. You have accepted reality, the Great Reality inside of you. Accepting that love in all situations is the answer to every concern. It means you recognize the God within. With God, all things are possible.

God is love. Love is the greatest force in the Universes and miracles can and do occur when this force is employed. Love one another as God loves you and all will be well. To integrate fully with your higher aspects, your human ego requires your love and compassion too.

Let your light shine more, and more. Welcome it. Understand the empowerment and great gift that it brings to everyone. Continue to celebrate, and stay in high vibration. That is the 'High Road' to Ascension that is ultimately what we all came to do.

If something appears in your consciousness, there is a reason. It may show you that there is another way. Visions and dreams reveal that you have the power to fix what is broken and heal what hurts. They catapult you beyond seeing with just your physical senses. Veils lift that keep you from seeing that you are already the person you dreamed you could be. You have just lived in a fantasy and illusion for too long.

When you awaken, you will have infinite knowledge, bringing you infinite peace and infinite joy. You will then be aware of all the possibilities available to you. You will be self-motivated to exercise your unique individual creative talents for your constant enjoyment and to share with others. Because all are one, each of us will delight in and fully enjoy the creations of everyone else. Fabulous and endless creative opportunities await all of us in a harmonious environment into which you are awakening.

Those behind the scenes who would keep us in the dense negative energy of the third dimension have tried to use the 2012 prophecies as some kind of end time's planetary disaster, rather than the end of the world of ego's fear. It is time to surrender your ego to God and awaken into joy. 2012 is the beginning of a grand new phase for humanity as it launches its climb out of ignorance and darkness into enlightenment and love.

Let your light shine to dispel the darkness and illuminate those around you. When you see the God in others, you are seeing your reflection of the Father within. The Father and I are one. He is our only Father. We become alive in spirit as we are transformed.

All you see is the goodness in all and God's spirit in all. All there is, is God. You are one with God. All there is, is love. Welcome home to the Great Reality. You have come home to your inheritance as a Child of God. It was always deep inside. You never left home. You claim your inheritance of unconditional love, abundance, and prosperity for eternity.

Then, Peace on Earth, and Goodwill towards all people will be possible. Sacred love expands when the divine in one person appreciates and honors the divine in another. Thus, the sacred wheel of love is created, and Heaven on Earth will manifest for those individuals. As this happens for everyone, Peace on Earth will become a reality.

Life is Love: Affirmations for Living

By Marilyn Redmond

It is okay to be one with God!
It's okay to feel good.
It's okay to enjoy love.
It's okay to share love.
It's okay to move in love.
It's okay to express love.
It's okay to experience love.
It's okay to be filled with love
It's okay to allow love to flow in my life
It's okay to have love flow through me, for my health.
It's okay to have love nurture me.
It's okay to thrive in love.
It's okay to create in love.
It's okay to allow love.
It's okay to live in love.
It's okay to give love.
It's okay to be love.
It's okay to accept the great present of love.

Perfection

By Marilyn Redmond

    Why does this painful past persevere
    withholding a pattern now permitted?
    Please reveal the source of your resistance
    Old beliefs, issues, ideas, stop persistence.
    Time for illusions to fade, slowly
    into perennial rainbows and pots of gold.
    An open heart is permanent devotion.
    Truth, light, bliss in eternal illumination.

    Balance permeates every particle. It flows
    peacefully right through your whole soul.
    Permanent protection fills within as pianos
    play harmoniously in ceaseless crescendos.

    Permissive energy performs affirmative
    persuasions. Grace tenderly attentive, is
    a precious moment, a pause in time,
    perpetuates premier agreement divine.

Afterward

Since writing this book, I have continued to teach, lecture, and write about this information at various engagements and platforms even though the 2012 date has passed. This information deals with the root cause of the issues in our lives and that there is a solution to resolve their recreating repeatedly. Ultimately, it is the answer to ending reincarnation because you heal your karma.

In verse 17 of 2 Corinthians, chapter 5, Therefore if any man be in Christ, he is a new creature: old things are passed away; behold all things are become new" becomes real as told in the Bible.

As you move into a higher consciousness, this is called the Christ consciousness that is demonstrated by Jesus in the New Testament. In addition, he did overcome the ego when he died to his lower emotions as in Mark 8, v.33," But when he had turned about and looked on his disciples, he rebuked Peter, saying, Get thee behind me, Satan: for thou savourest not the things that be of God, but the things that be of men." In this quote, he rose above the mentality of the duality of good and bad—a human dimension. He saw everything from unconditional love and forgiveness—Christ-Consciousness.

In addition, many famous people that are not religious have told us this information in varying testimony, evidence, and demonstrations over the years. Edgar Cayce, the great psychic of the twentieth century, often in his spiritual readings states that the body, mind, and soul are lower vibrations of the earth and a material world and the Christ-

Consciousness, the Holy Spirit and your guardian angels bear witness in a higher spirit.

Albert Einstein said that no problem could be solved from the same level of consciousness that created it. Therefore, raising your consciousness will bring a new realization. It is as simple as moving from the ego into a perception of unconditional love.

Even channeled information shares this in a different awareness. "You simply cannot co-create with the universal (LOVE) intelligence from the energy of, the vibration of, lack. If there is anything in your world that you "think" you are lacking, you are….by the physics of creation. Stay awake to this truth, and you will fare well." *Pleiadian High Council*

Knowing that the ego offers lack in your life based in fear, not focusing on this level of thinking brings an understanding that releasing the ego brings solutions and fulfillment. I hope that all who read this book apply this information. Different results will emerge. The outcome will bring the peace for which everyone has been praying for hundreds of years—Heaven on Earth.

www.ingramcontent.com/pod-product-compliance
Lightning Source LLC
Chambersburg PA
CBHW060220050426
42446CB00013B/3121